S0-BMU-957

Horatio
The Man Who Saved a City

By Pauline Cartwright

Illustrated by Francis Phillipps

⌐⊃ Dominie Press, Inc.

Publisher: Raymond Yuen
Project Editor: John S. F. Graham
Editor: Bob Rowland
Designer: Greg DiGenti
Illustrator: Francis Phillipps

Text Copyright © 2003 Pauline Cartwright
Illustrations Copyright © 2003 Dominie Press, Inc.
All rights reserved. No part of this publication may
be reproduced or transmitted in any form or by any
means without permission in writing from the publisher.
Reproduction of any part of this book, through photocopy,
recording, or any electronic or mechanical retrieval system,
without the written permission of the publisher, is an
infringement of the copyright law.

Published by:

𝄞 Dominie Press, Inc.

1949 Kellogg Avenue
Carlsbad, California 92008 USA

www.dominie.com

1-800-232-4570

Paperback ISBN 0-7685-1623-4
Printed in Singapore
  11 12 13 14 V0ZF 14 13

Table of Contents

Italy,
about 400 B.C.

Tiber River

Etruscan

Roman

In the early days of Rome,
before it was an empire
to be admired and feared,
the Etruscan army and
the Roman army fought
each other for years. They
were just two of many
small states around the
Mediterranean Sea that
were constantly at war
with one another.

Chapter One

A Large and Frightening Army

Horatio, an officer in the Roman army, was one of the people who heard the watchmen shout their warning.

"The Etruscans are coming! The Etruscans are coming!"

The Romans felt fear run through

their bodies, from head to toe. They raced to high ground, on tall buildings and hills, to see for themselves whether it was really true. Then, seeing the mighty Etruscan army approaching, they fled to their homes and shut themselves inside.

Everyone feared the Etruscans. They had a large and frightening army, which had threatened the Romans before. Only the Tiber River separated Rome from the fierce and clever Etruscan warriors.

When Horatio realized he could hear the army, he was worried. How had they come so close before the watchmen saw them coming? If the Etruscans had been seen early enough, the Roman army could have crossed the river and met them. Then they could have prevented their enemies from reaching the river and taking command of the bridge.

Horatio knew it was too late for that now. They had been taken by surprise. He hurried—with the few soldiers who were nearby—to gather weapons and put on armor.

As they assembled in their ranks, they listened with dread to the tread of many marching feet, and to the clank of armor. At any moment, the Etruscans could take command of the bridge. Then they would pour into Rome!

Chapter Two
The Bridge

Horatio was thinking hard as he picked up his armored vest. And suddenly he knew what to do. He ran to join his unit without worrying about the rest of his armor.

By now, everyone could hear the

commands being shouted by the enemy, and they could see the mass of soldiers on the other side of the bridge. The noisy rattle of soldiers assembling made it hard for one person to be heard.

But Horatio shouted to whoever could hear. "The Etruscans can only get into our city by crossing the bridge. If there is no bridge, they can't cross the Tiber! We must cut it down!"

Some soldiers nearby heard him and were amazed.

"Cut it down?" they asked.

"Cut down the bridge!"

"It's too late for that!" they said. "They could get across before we could finish cutting it!"

"No!" cried Horatio. "It isn't too late! With their armor and weapons, only one—two at the most—can cross the bridge at a time! Don't you see? I could stop them by myself!"

Some soldiers who heard only his last words stopped buckling on their armor to hoot with laughter.

"Well then, what do we need our swords for?" they shouted.

"Go ahead, friend! Stop the enemy. Save us a job!"

But two soldiers, Titus and Spurius, pushed through the milling Roman soldiers. As others jeered and scoffed at Horatio, the two ran quickly to his side.

Then, as Horatio ran from the ranks and across the bridge, they ran, too.

Chapter Three
Advance!

When Horatio saw Titus and Spurius running to help him, he was heartened. Although he didn't have all his protective armor on, he was ready to do combat with just his sword and shield.

Horatio took up a position on one

end of the bridge. Titus and Spurius stood just behind him.

On the other side of the Tiber, the Etruscan troops quickly got in line to come over the bridge. Horatio saw the wicked glint of many drawn swords. He saw the fierceness on the faces of the enemy. But the Etruscans barely noticed him—or his friends. They had come to the very edge of the Tiber without being seen by the Romans, and their eyes were on the prize of the mighty city of Rome! Nothing was going to stop them now.

A leader's cry rang out, "Advance!"

A line of soldiers began running onto the bridge. Horatio's sword flashed. The first man fell and toppled into the Tiber below. The second man fell. The third managed to run past. Horatio's companions stopped the Etruscan warrior and threw him over the side.

"Advance! Advance!"

Horatio cut down another man, and another. He was glad he had not taken time to put on all his armor. Wielding his sword was easier without a lot of metal on his arms. One approaching Etruscan soldier fled suddenly, simply because of the confident smile on Horatio's face.

Behind and below Horatio and his friends, the sound of ax blows was unheard by the enemy. It was drowned out by the Etruscans' rallying cries and by the ringing of clashing swords. But Horatio, Titus, and Spurius understood what needed to be done. The bridge was going to fall with them on it.

Chapter Four
Only Three Men

Below the three men holding back the enemy, other soldiers of the Roman army were swinging axes that cut through the timbers of the bridge. More soldiers were tying ropes around the supports, straining and pulling so that great slabs of wood began to teeter and sway.

The Etruscans kept coming. They didn't realize that the bridge supports were being smashed away. They saw only Rome—and three men in the way. Three men weren't going to stop an invasion! Nothing was going to stop them now. *Nothing!*

"They can't fight forever. Three swords can't kill an entire army," muttered one Etruscan officer.

"The arms that hold the swords will grow tired," said another. "They can't hold the bridge forever."

The words made the next man feel strong, and he ran onto the bridge, flailing his sword wildly. Horatio felled him, and the one who followed, and the one after that. The few who slipped past him were felled by Titus and Spurius.

By this time, the Etruscans at the front of the ranks had taken their eyes off of Rome and put them instead on the man and his friends who stood in their path. Three men—*only three men*—stood in their way, and their strong and mighty army couldn't pass! How could this be?

But the Etruscans still didn't look below the bridge. They had no idea what was happening there.

Suddenly a voice from the other side of the bridge called to Horatio. "Now! Now!"

Glancing backward, Horatio and his friends saw that nearly all of the bridge supports had been chopped through and pulled apart. Only a single plank of timber kept the bridge in place. They could feel the cracking of wood beneath their feet.

"Go!" cried Horatio to his friends. "Go now!"

While Horatio continued to wield his sword fiercely, Titus and Spurius turned and ran to safety, the planks and supports creaking and cracking beneath their feet.

Chapter Five
One Tug of a Rope

The Etruscans suddenly saw what was happening. For a moment, soldiers stopped running toward the bridge.

Horatio leaped off the bridge and onto the Etruscan side of the river to stand boldly in front of the enemy soldiers.

They stared at him. What was happening now?

Behind him, Horatio heard the blow of an ax. He knew that one tug of a rope meant the last swaying bridge support would be gone. All at once, the rope was pulled, and the bridge cracked and crumbled, tumbling down into the river.

Into the startled faces of the enemy, Horatio cried, "Rome is ours! *Ours!*" He knew the plan had worked. No Etruscans would pour into his city now. The surprise attack was foiled. Rome was safe.

The Etruscans were shocked and fuming. Their entire army had been defeated by one man. They had him now. With no bridge for his retreat, Horatio was cornered at the edge of the Tiber.

But as they took a few steps toward

Horatio, he threw his sword and shield aside, leaped into the river, and swam for his home shore.

The furious Etruscans—their prize only a few yards away—were left stranded. They couldn't follow Horatio into the river, because their armor would weigh them down. Rome was untouchable.

That night, the Romans held great celebrations. The wit and courage of one man had saved the city of Rome from destruction.

The story of his courage was told for years to come. It told, too, of how Horatio was given a reward—as much land as he could plow around in one day. And in one of their temples his grateful fellow citizens erected a statue of him with this inscription: *Horatio, defender of the bridge, defender of Rome.*

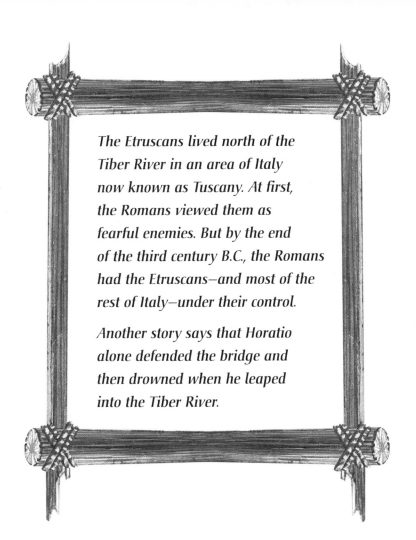

The Etruscans lived north of the Tiber River in an area of Italy now known as Tuscany. At first, the Romans viewed them as fearful enemies. But by the end of the third century B.C., the Romans had the Etruscans—and most of the rest of Italy—under their control.

Another story says that Horatio alone defended the bridge and then drowned when he leaped into the Tiber River.